of Castello

A Hymn to Her Life
1287-1320 AD

Edited by:
Fabrio Bricca
Gianni Festa, OP

NEW PRIORY PRESS

2021

Table of Contents

Introduction

fr. Gianni Festa, OP
General Postulator

[...]
With my hands I touch the walls
But with my soul the truth,
My fingers dark for me
But God, a flare.

What is distant I feel to be close
When I think, I believe I define;
My body sitting in today,
My soul wavers in the infinite.

Graceful things from the air
Come for my orchestrations.
I hear only birds' wings
But I see the wings of angels.

Sometimes I sing without a voice,
Just as I think without speaking
The blindness God has given me
Is a way of giving me light.

If I proceed along the way
My pathways are two:
One, where I am walking,
The other, the truth in which I am.

In me there is, at the bottom of a well,
An opening of light towards God.
There, at the very bottom,
An eye made in heaven.[1]

This lyric poem by the Portuguese poet Fernando Pessoa, which I came upon by chance in an anthology given to me by a nun friend and which turned up "by chance" on my desk, seems to be the perfect expression of the Christian, spiritual experience of Blessed Margherita della Metola (the town of Mercatello sul Metauro) or of Città di Castello. Hers was a short life, passed in the evocative surroundings of the Massa Tribaria and Tifernum (the old name for Città di Casrello), though contemplation of their beauty was denied her because she was blind from birth until her death in 1320. These verses which, in the development of their light quatrains, aim at the theological depth of the obstructed relationship between outer blindness and inner light or gaze seem to be particularly apt for a commentary on the text of the two *legendae* which, in different ways and variations, insist on the stylistic element of "providential blindness": she was blind, but she saw the light.

I recall only a few of the passages in which the author of the *Vita lunga* remarks, with theological perspicacity and scriptural inspiration, on the deprivation of sight as

---

1. Fernando Pessoa, Sono un sogno di Dio (Magnano (BI): Qiqajon, 2015), 53.

an "intervention of Providence": "In fact she was born without bodily eyes so as not to see the world, but she took her fill of the divine light because, while on the earth, she could contemplate only heaven."[2] (Pessoa writes "The blindness God has given me / Is a way of giving me light."[3]) When her parents took her to Città di Castello to pray that she be healed by a Franciscan friar who had recently died in odour of sanctity, they were to be disappointed because "the Lord, having already illuminated her mind with the wish to contemplate the heavenly realities, did not want to satisfy them—He who knows all secrets—so that she should not be deprived, by the sight of earthly things, of the vision of heavenly things";[4] and once left (or abandoned) alone and mendicant in the streets of the Tifernum town, "she who was considered abandoned was at once welcomed by God, [and] while separated from the world was illuminated by the eternal light, that her mind might be raised to meditate more freely on the eternal realities."[5] At a later point in the text, the hagiographer raises his voice to proclaim Margaret's teaching charism, which was, yes, a feminine teaching, humble and delicate, but undoubtedly evangelical in tone: "Blessed blind woman,

---

2. Vita lunga della Beata Margherita (Recensio major, BHL 5313az), in Le vite dei santi di Città di Castello nel Medioevo, ed. P. Liccardello (Selci-Lama, Italy: Editrice Pliniana, 2017), 251.

3. Pessoa, Sono un sogno di Dio, 53.

4. Vita lunga, 253.

5. Ibid.

I say, who never saw the things of this world and who so quickly learned heavenly things! Happy disciple, who deserved to have such a master, who without books taught Holy Scripture to you, blind from birth, who teach even those who can see."[6] Despite being able to "see nothing," nevertheless with that "eye made in heaven,"[7] she contemplated the invisible made visible, the Incarnate, God made man, present in the Eucharist.

In Church, when the Body of our Lord Jesus Christ was consecrated and throughout the time when the sacred mystery was celebrated, she claimed that she saw Christ incarnate[8] and that she could see nothing else going on (*actualiter*). It is no wonder that he who had deprived her of any sight of earthly things wanted to show himself

---

6. Ibid., 261

7. Pessoa, *Sono un sogno di Dio*, 53.

8. Anne Lécu, a Dominican Sister who has worked for years as a doctor in French prisons, when recalling the martyrdom of Father Jacques Hamel—killed by two militant members of fundamentalist Islam on July 26, 2016, while he was celebrating Mass in the church of St. Etienne du Rouvray in Normandy—offers an unusually effective summary of theological expression on the vital bond between the person who takes part and believes in the Eucharist and Christ as really present in the bread and wine: "The Eucharist, inasmuch as it is a summary of the most ordinary life of the believers, is the place where we are configured to Christ and where, by the grace of those who participate, the world is configured to Christ, incarnate, crucified, risen." Anne Lécu and Valerio Lanzarini, *Una vita donata* (Magnano (BI): Qiqajon, 2018), 6.

only to her pure gaze, so that in an earthenware vessel of little value, divine mercy should shine forth.[9]

Like Christ who gave himself up for love of humanity, so Margaret did with her own life, apparently insignificant and superfluous to worldly "eyes," a "life of gift."

The metaphor of the "earthenware vessel," is taken from St. Paul:

> But we have this treasure in earthen vessels, to show that the transcendent power belongs to God and not to us. We are afflicted in every way, but not crushed; perplexed, but not driven to despair; persecuted, but not forsaken; struck down, but not destroyed; always carrying in the body the death of Jesus, so that the life of Jesus may also be manifested in our bodies.[10]

This metaphor cannot fail to remind us of a famous passage from the Apostle which sheds ample light on the meaning of Margaret's life and holiness:

> For consider your call, brethren; not many of you were wise according to worldly standards, not many were powerful, not many were of noble birth; but God chose what is foolish in the world to shame the wise, God chose what is weak in the world to shame the strong, God chose what is low and despised in the world, even things that are not, to bring to nothing

---

9. Vita lunga, 261.
10. 2 Cor. 4:7–10.

things that are, so that no human being might boast in the presence of God.[11]

Once more, as I have often happened to recall in other institutional and/or more official venues, I am aware of an inner, deeply felt need to say again, with inspired conviction, that the newness of the fame of holiness and the vigour of the cult of Margaret are not to be attributed to a sort of artificial discovery or archaeological recovery of a mediaeval Blessed but rather to a manifestation of the Spirit of God that works in history and that mysteriously and often invisibly ferments the dough of humanity with the yeast of its surprising dynamism. The fact is that the fame of Margaret's holiness and her cult have never ceased, and if, at least until the nineteenth century, they were for the most part confined to Italy and within the Dominican Order, they have spread with unforeseen growth thanks to the religious men and women of the Dominican Family to all over the world. Our little Margaret still lives in the hearts and prayers of many of the faithful, not only in Umbria and the Marches but also in the USA and in the Philippines. The present vitality of her cult, the extraordinary spread of her fame in countries far distant from Città di Castello or Metola, the freshness of her pathway of perfection, and the exemplary nature of her poor life bear witness to the fact that still today Margaret can speak to the hearts of thousands of men and women because in her they recognise a sister, one of their own,

---

11. 1 Cor. 1:26–29.

one of those humble, blessed creatures whom one day, exulting in the Spirit, Jesus indicated as the only keepers of true wisdom: "I thank you, Father, Lord of heaven and earth, because you have hidden these things from the wise and the intelligent and have revealed them to infants; yes, Father, for such was your gracious will."[12]

---

12. Luke 10:21.

Blessed and Beautiful

fr. Gerard Francisco Timoner III, OP
Master of the Order

"He had no majestic bearing to catch our eye, no beauty to draw us to him."[13] Ordinarily, we seek the intercession of saints for our special needs or intentions. We pray that they may have mercy on our plight so that they may aid us by their prayers, and we hope for a miracle.

In 1986, when I was a novice at Santo Domingo Convent in Quezon City, Philippines, I was struck by the image of Blessed Margaret of Castello. Her statue is not like that of the beautiful St. Rose of Lima or St. Catherine of Siena. She was blind and hunchbacked, on a pedestal by the door of the huge church, as though hesitant to come close to the altar because of her disfigured looks. But many people are drawn to her not because they seek *from* her the compassionate intercession of a miraculous saint but because they "feel compassion" *for* her, not in a condescending way, but because they identify with her. Many Filipinos love "suffering heroes." Perhaps this explains partly why she has so many devotees. The life story of Blessed Margaret of Castello is almost like a soap opera: she was born blind, had severe curvature of the spine, one of her legs was shorter than the other, one arm was malformed, she was unloved by her parents, hidden from other people, rejected and later abandoned

---

13. Is. 53:2.

12

by her family, and then she found a new family among the Dominican sisters who welcomed her and loved her unconditionally.

But even if she seemed in need of corporal works of mercy due to her physical disability, Blessed Margaret performed inspiring corporal works of mercy: she nursed the sick, consoled the dying, and visited prisoners. She was like that poor widow in the parable told by Jesus who gave generously even if she had almost nothing.[14] Blessed Margaret loved with a magnanimous heart even if she was unloved as a child. Truly, she was a "wounded healer," a person with disability who enabled people to become better, a rejected one who welcomed the dejected; indeed, she was a **beautiful image** of God's transforming love.

In Blessed Margaret, the wise words of the beautiful movie actress Audrey Hepburn became a reality: "For beautiful eyes, look for the **good** in others; for beautiful lips, speak only words of **kindness**; and for poise, walk with the knowledge that **you are never alone.**" Blessed Margaret was blind but she *saw* the goodness in people; she was born with a structural leg length discrepancy, but she walked with grace because she knew that she was walking humbly in God's presence.

In the following pages of this book dedicated to Margherita di Citta di Castello, the 7th centenary of whose birth into eternal life we celebrated in the year

---

14. See Luke 21:1–4.

2020, we will discover more profoundly her enduring *beauty* and *blessedness*.

The Life of Blessed Margaret "The Blind Woman of the Metola"

Fabio Bricca

According to the fourteenth-century biographies, Blessed Margaret was born in 1287[15] to Parisio and Emilia in the castle of Metola,[16] which was ruled by her father and situated in the territory of Mercatello on the Metauro river in the southern area of the ancient region of Massa Trabaria.[17] She was born "small and deformed," totally blind and with dysmetria of her lower limbs which made her lame. She was baptised in the old parish church of San Pietro d'Ico, today Mercatello. The aristocratic family did not accept the child's disability, which made her unfit for anything and hence a useless burden; they reacted with shame and rejection.

---

15. Scholars have usually fixed her birth in 1287. See E. GiovaGnoli, *Vita della beata Margherita da Città di Castello, Terziaria domenicana*, (Città di Castello: Tipografia Petruzzi, reissue 1997), 12. See also W. R. Bonniwel, *Margherita di Città di Castello, Vivere nella luce* (Rome: Città Nuova Editrice, reissue 2002), 19.

16. Cf. U. Valentini, Beata Margherita della Metola, Una sfida all'emarginazione (Città di Castello: Tipografia Petruzzi, 1988), 295–297.

17. The earliest biographies of Blessed Margaret date back to the second half of the fourteenth century. See P. Licciardello, Le vite dei santi di Città di Castello (Selci Lama: Editrice Pliniana, 2017), 238–321.

When she was still a small child, perhaps partly with the intention of protecting her, they transferred her to a sort of walled cell with a single small window that looked out on an oratory and through which they passed her food. This was the opportunity for the start of a powerful spiritual journey on the model of the so-called "imprisoned women" under the guidance of the parish priest of the castle. She remained in this prison for some time, very occasionally visited by her mother, while the chaplain instructed her in Scripture, prayer, and liturgy and introduced her to sacramental life and to the loftiest mysteries of faith.

She devoted herself to penitential practices, fasting on bread and water every Friday and abstaining from meat throughout the year; as a child she began wearing a cilice, which she concealed out of prudence and humility. In this period of isolation, she refined her ascetic abilities and progressed in her knowledge of faith, learning total trust in Providence and cultivating the expiatory value of acceptance of suffering in union with Christ. The Lord was preparing her for her life's mission: to bring the good news to the oppressed, to bind up the broken hearted.[18]

As a girl, after a period spent in Mercatello for her greater safety in view of the continual fighting among the various local lords to conquer the small fort of Metola, Margaret was taken by her parents to Città di Castello to pray at the tomb of Brother Giacomo (James), a revered

---

18. Cf. Is. 61:1.

Franciscan, in the hope of obtaining healing through his intercession.

There was no miracle, and the noble chatelaines of the Metola, as though to challenge Providence and as they were unable to guide their daughter into a plausible life plan, abandoned her there with the burden of her fragile human condition. Alone and with no material support, she lived as a beggar, the guest of the city's poor families, until she was admitted to the monastery of Santa Margaret.

She was sent away from this monastery because her ascetic strictness and her perfect adherence to the Gospel conflicted with the laid-back practices of the community. Young as she was, she was able to suffer public disdain and her "failure" to accede to religious life, thus experiencing a second abandonment.

On leaving the monastery, she settled in the home of Venturino and Grigia, where she found a loving family capable of appreciating her human qualities (they gave her domestic work) and indulging in her spiritual tendencies. According to some sources, she was taken in for some time by devout persons even before the period when she had lived in the monastery.

Through Donna Grigia, in 1301 when she was about 14, Margaret of Metola was admitted in the church of La Carità to the Mantellate, devout laywomen connected to the Friars Precahers/Dominicans who lived in their own homes but faithfully followed the Rule and wore the Dominican habit—white tunics and black cloaks—during liturgical celebrations and acts of public worship. In the wealthy home of Venturino, she had asked to be allowed to live in a ghastly room in the attic, with no creature comforts, and there she had led a life of intense prayer and penance. She spent entire nights in prayer, with brief periods of rest.

She was highly regarded in the town for her spirituality and for the joy she was able to instil in those who met her while her great knowledge of the Holy Scriptures, even though she could not read, roused amazement. Her faith life was also centered on her daily attendance at the Sacrament of Penance and at Mass. She made her communion as often as she was granted permission by her confessor, and during the elevation she "saw" the Child Jesus in the consecrated host. During prayer or liturgical celebrations, she was often seized by profound mystical ecstasies accompanied by levitation. She daily recited the Office of the Cross, the Psalms (all of which she knew by heart), and the Office of the Virgin Mary, to whom she was particularly devoted.

She regularly meditated on episodes in the life of the Holy Family such as the Virgin's giving birth in Bethlehem, the flight into Egypt, and Joseph's loving service to Jesus and Mary. So ardent and continuous was her contemplation of these holy mysteries that they were literally stamped on her heart as was discovered after her death when, during an identification of her body, there were found within her heart three precious stones representing a child between two farm animals (the Nativity), the Virgin with her crown, and St. Joseph—white-bearded and cloaked—with a woman in the

Dominican habit kneeling at his feet. These sacred images recall the humble, joyful words Margaret so often spoke: "Oh, if you knew the treasure I have in my heart you would marvel at it." The church authorities themselves had respect for her teaching, united as it was to an exemplary life and to a passionate evangelising endeavour. Her spirituality, then, is of a mystico-penitential nature, and one may say that her spiritual life was Christiform, i.e., constantly conformed to Christ.

It was from this profound contemplative life that she drew inspiration and strength for an intense apostolate of mercy which brought her into contact with the wretched of every kind. Her life was enriched with valuable experiences in contact with the social reality of the town to which she was introduced by Donna Grigia. Despite her disability, she went into the streets to care for the marginalised, the poor, and the sick, who were often healed by the power of her humble prayer or consoled by her benevolent conversation. She healed the eyes of one of her sisters in religion, showing that she who was blind from birth was in profound uniformity with the mysterious projects of divine love.

She worked to bring peace in families and to cheer the wretched conditions of convicts, comforting them in prison and instilling hope in the merciful fatherhood of God in them. Apropos this, her biographers relate an extraordinary fact: the story of a blasphemous prisoner who, when he saw her seized by ecstasy and levitating, was converted at the evidence of the divine power that was made manifest by the love of this tiny, blind servant of God. For all his fellow-citizens, he became a point of reference and a model of evangelical life poured out for the neediest and most abandoned of his neighbours.

On April 13, 1320, the second Sunday of Easter, at the age of 33, Margaret passed away, and the local population insisted that her body be buried in the church of La Carità, as was fitting for her holiness. Sometime after her death, remembering Margaret's words heard by Donna Grigia and by many Dominican religious, "Ah, if you knew what I have in my heart!", it was decided to examine her cardiac muscle in the presence of the authorities, doctors, aristocrats, and devout persons, so the vessel containing her heart—removed after her death and preserved in a suitable container—was opened. The cardiac muscle was found to be intact. Found in it were three spheres bearing the images of the Child Jesus, Mary, and St. Joseph, the crib she had always loved and meditated on.

The body was later moved under the main altar of the Church of San Domenico in Città di Castello where it has rested, uncorrupted, for 700 years, honoured by the Lord with the granting of graces and venerated by the faithful and by pilgrims.

Thus the "blind woman of Metola," the rejected stone, has become a glory of the Church, a true pillar (*metula*) supporting the needy and the marginalised, giving hope and consolation to the imperfect, the humble, and the defenceless. The Lord granted this mission to Margaret, who was a victim of rejection and abandonment, who experienced the failure of sympathy from her parents, who suffered prejudices, who lived with sickness and forms of dependence that were always with her, but who was able to rise above them and indeed take advantage of them in the light of the Easter mystery in which every suffering and every cross is transformed into life and resurrection.

The *"Lives"* of Blessed Margaret

Andrea Czortek

The primary source for knowledge of Blessed Margaret is the two *Lives*, probably written in Città di Castello between 1347 and 1400: the so-called *Long Life* is attributed to a canon of the Cathedral and the other, the *Short Life*, to a Dominican friar. The author of the *Long Life* was able to consult an older biography and the collection of miracles compiled by the notaries after Margaret's death.

Scholars are convinced of the substantial historical reliability of the two texts, as they were written shortly after the facts they narrate, facts held to be plausible, from her birth in or around 1287 to her death on April 13, 1320.

Various circumstances described in these *Lives* help us to understand certain important aspects of religious life and society in Città di Castello and the Apennine region in Umbria and the Marches in the thirteenth and fourteenth centuries. These texts are of special value for the religious history of a period characterised by a notable female presence in the life of the Church. This presence took various forms and was often supported by the Franciscans and the Dominicans. Margaret herself, during her life, experienced a variety of conditions: individual reclusion, life in a monastery, and admission to the Dominican Third Order. These forms of life were widespread in mediaeval cities and point to the powerful awakening of religious awareness that was characteristic of the thirteenth and fourteenth centuries, the pursuit of liberty (as compared with older, more institutionalised regular forms), and an assessment of the female state that sought autonomous, original ways of responding to the spiritual demands of the time.

These fourteenth century *Lives*, in speaking of Margaret, tell us of various devotional aspects of her time such as fasting, daily prayer, confession, and participation in Mass. As regards to her death, they stress the phenomenon of civic piety, expressed in veneration for a woman who belonged to the local society and was already considered a saint in her lifetime. The two hagiographic texts, translated into Italian by Pierluigi Licciardello in 2017, speak not only of Margaret but of her times; they present the human and spiritual experience of a woman in the Middle Ages and also help us to reconstruct certain significant expressions of Christian faith characterising one of the most dynamic, fertile cultural and social periods in the history of this Apennine community. It was a period when the valleys on either side of the mountains were enlivened by the presence of nobles and merchants, monks and friars, artists and intellectuals, and peasants and artisans: among them all, the choice of history has fallen on little Margaret to offer us an exemplary life of hope and love that speaks to us still today.

The Cult of Blessed Margaret

Andrea Czortek and Fabio Bricca

Veneration of Blessed Margaret developed in Città di Castello immediately after her death, when—as the fourteenth-century *Lives* tell us—the local people demanded that she be buried in the church. In 1395, a chapel was built in the Dominicans' new church with an altar bearing the name of "St. Margherita of Citta di Castello" (thus the notary's document), and there is a reference to the celebration of a feast with exposition of her body. After the present church of San Domenico was built, the body was moved there in 1424 and then was given canonical recognition in 1588. In 1604, Pope Clement VIII granted an indulgence to those who should visit Margaret's body, and in 1609 her liturgical cult was approved. Later, in 1743, 1769, and 1844, the body was recognised.

The cult of Blessed Margaret underwent great development at the beginning of the twentieth century when, in view of the sixth centenary of her death in 1920, Canon Giacinto Faeti promoted the restoration of the church of San Domenico—transformed into a sanctuary devoted to Margaret—and the foundation of an institute for the blind with the name of "the Blind Woman of Metola." In 1987 and 1988, the seventh centenary of her birth was celebrated with religious and cultural enterprises.

Her cult is still lively today both in the town and throughout the diocese not least because of the annual celebration of the obligatory memoria fixed on May 4 by the diocesan liturgical calendar approved in 1981. In 1998, her body underwent canonical recognition, and in 2000, the diocesan inquiry "super culto a saeculo XIV tributo," in view of her canonisation. This inquiry ended in September 2004.

On April 27, 1718, Pope Clement XI (who was from Urbania) approved the Mass and Office of Blessed Margaret for the Diocese of Urbania and Sant'Angelo in Vado where her cult and devotion to the little saint spread, especially in Mercatello sul Metauro and at Sant'Angelo in Vado. There were also manifestations of devotion in Urbania, which was the diocesan centre of the Vicariate of Mercatello. The liturgical calendar of the Archdiocese of Urbino-Urbania-Sant'Angelo in Vado celebrates her memoria on April 13, the date on which she died.

Veneration of Margaret is particularly intense in Mercatello on the River Metauro and is shown in some circumstances with a special, assiduous public veneration and with the dedication of certain places. On the second Sunday of Easter, there is a special memorial of Margaret in the Collegiate parish church where she was baptised. Vespers is followed by a procession with a statue and relics of Blessed Margaret. On September 22, 1957, a shrine was inaugurated with a marble statue from Vicenza that was commissioned by the citizens of Mercatello and erected in the gardens that bear her name. This statue looks towards Metola, where she was born. Mercatello has also named a road after its famous daughter—Via Beata Margherita della Metola—which links the historic center of the town with the church of the Madonna of the Metauro and the cemetery.

On May 1 in the church of Santo Stefano in Metola, the feast in honour of Margaret is celebrated with Mass and a procession.

On the second Sunday in August, the parish of San Michele Arcangelo in Sant'Angelo in Vado organises a pilgrimage on foot to the oratory of Blessed Margaret, where Mass is celebrated. This place has recently been enhanced thanks to the praiseworthy initiative of several of the faithful and is a constant destination of pilgrimages and prayer meetings.

In April 1988, the seventh centenary of Margaret's birth was celebrated in Mercatello with the presence of Cardinal Pietro Palazzini and a week of celebrations and pastoral initiatives.

On October 26, 1988, at the request of the Archbishop of Urbino-Urbania-Sant'Angelo in Vado, Msgr. Ugo Donato Bianchi, and the Bishop of Città di Castelo, Msgr. Carlo Urru, the Congregation for Divine Worship nominated her Patron with the Lord of those usually called "sightless" and "outcasts" for their respective dioceses. Both Mercatello on the Metauro and Sant'Angelo in Vado host associations in honour of Blessed Margaret of Metola, and these promote her cult and awareness of her.

There is an association in her honour in the parish of St. Patrick in Columbus, Ohio, where in the parish church, a shrine has been built in her honour with a statue in wood portraying her handicaps, namely that she was blind, lame, and walked with a stick. "Little Margaret's Charity" is a charitable organisation to help the poor and in support of life.

There is a shrine devoted to her in the church of St. Louis Bertrand in Louisville, Kentucky. Her cult is promoted in the church of St. Catherine of Siena in Manhattan, New York. The year 1985 saw the birth of a center of national worship with a chapel and statue of Margaret in the church of the Holy Name of Jesus in Philadelphia, Pennsylvania. Various associations bearing her name and connected with these churches are engaged on various projects of assistance to support outcasts, prevent abortion, and help the poor. In Downsview, Canada, a kindergarten and elementary school bear the name of Margaret, as does a house that offers support to pregnant women in difficulty.

The cult of Blessed Margaret is widespread in the Philippines, where in 1987 a spiritual movement arose in the church of St. Dominic in Quezon City where her liturgical feast happens on April 13 and a weekly prayer meeting occurs. Here, too, an association was born that has made Margaret a symbol of pro-life activities and of championing the handicapped. The "Pro-Life Philippines Foundation" counts her among its patrons.

Love of this blind woman of Metola is also taking root in Australia, Mexico, Japan, and India.

Margaret,
Mystic of the Heart of God

Alessandra Bartolomei

The long history of Christian holiness numbers among its protagonists many great women, some very famous, others less well known. But how can we explain the extraordinary devotion that has for centuries surrounded Blessed Margaret? How is it possible that this mediaeval cult, rather than being extinguished, has gradually increased and has by now crossed borders far from its original home, the Apennine territories of Umbria and the Marches, reaching the distant Philippines and the Americas? What is the universal meaning of her testimony?

Margaret of Città di Castello did nothing exceptional unlike Hildegrade of Bingen and Catherine of Siena, who were politically active and turned the power of their charism on popes and great sovereigns; she founded no congregations unlike Clare of Assisi and Teresa of Avila; she wrote no memorable books unlike Angela of Foligno. This Dominican "Mantellata" led a simple, hidden life between her domestic cell and the church, a life of penitence and prayer and hence apparently without important events. But her *Legenda*, in the etymological sense of "something to read" (Latin *legere*), takes us in all its essential nature and clarity to an original truth of Christianity, to that ancient blessing[19] which, inverting the roles, delivers the divine lesson to the poor, the little ones, and not to the great men of the world.[20]

Ubertino of Casale understood this: this great Franciscan spiritual figure came down from the pulpit to listen to this woman who lived close to the heart of Jesus, permeated with his suffering, and who, held close in God's embrace, united with Him, and taught Ubertino true wisdom—a wisdom that is not learned in the world's academies but at the school of Christ. Ubertino was a very learned man, but he wrote that Margaret was his teacher more than many theological and speculative scholars. At a time of serious spiritual crisis, she had enlightened and supported him, giving him the strength to continue his work. It was she who taught him the way to know, love and truly imitate the life of Christ in order to follow in His footsteps.

But Margaret's spiritual greatness was understood too by the inhabitants of Città di Castello who at her death asked that she be buried in their church: they regarded her as a saint before she was recognised officially as such. As was customary at that time in such circumstances, her body was prepared for embalming, and that was when three small pearls were found in her heart bearing the images of three faces: the icons of Mary, Joseph, and the child Jesus, the members of the Holy Family. That was the moment that revealed the secret of the supernatural joy that Margaret had never

---

19. Cf. Matt. 18:1–10.
20. Cf. Luke 1:51–53.

lost in the face of the harshest trials of her life: blindness, sickness, and rejection. She was not the poor orphan of Metola because the Lord had never abandoned her, and she had been able to fill the gap left by her human family with the little crib that had always dwelt in her heart.

Some years earlier, in 1308, something similar had happened in Montefalco, an Umbrian town not far from Città di Castello. When their abbess, Clare, died, the nuns in her monastery opened her body and, in her heart, found the symbols of the Passion: the Cross, the scourge, and the pillar, while in her gall bladder they came upon three pearls of the same size, weight, and colour arranged in the form of a triangle like the symbol of the Trinity. We must not think of these episodes as a manifestation of the uncivilised, primitive, superstitious Middle Ages. Even at that time they provoked amazement and bewilderment.

When the news of this marvel of Clare spread, the authorities of Montefalco immediately opened an inquiry into the facts relating to the monastery: there were even inspectors sent from Rome to make sure that there had not been a cunning falsification by the nuns on a matter of supreme importance. The papal legate Berengario of Saint-Affrique not only personally checked that there had been no counterfeiting or trickery but was transformed into the most convinced supporter of Clare's holiness, writing her biography and promoting the cause of her canonisation. Twelve years later, there was no dramatic polarisation in Città di Castello between the opposing parties of sceptics and believers, which had caused that disturbance in the small town of Montefalco. How, then, are we to interpret the meaning of these astonishing miracles? To understand, we must adopt a symbolic viewpoint: the bodies of these women were not corpses, they were a writing surface, a desk-body that spoke of their lives, almost a talking Bible, engraved with the memory of the pains and sufferings of their lives. After all, this was the situation with Francis of Assisi at La Verna when his body had been pierced by the arrows of the Seraph.

The center of faith for Clare, mystical exegete of the Passion, was the crucified Christ; for Margaret it was the mystery of the Incarnation. Thus, through this miracle she entered the ranks of the *magistrae* of the *theologia cordis* with Lutgardis of Tongres, Gertrude of Helfta, Rose of Viterbo, and Clare of the Cross, mystics whose bodies were transparent as tabernacles like the *Vierges ouvrantes*, the wooden statues that flooded the piety and sacred art of the fourteenth century. Indeed, a tormented body was regularly to accompany the image of Blessed Margaret, an iconographic attribute that was to make her immediately recognisable even in the long processions of Dominican Saints and Blessed, all clothed in black and white, all with a lily in their hands. The little crib, almost a bequest, was the message given to Margaret: her spiritual eyes had been able to see, in her state of abandonment and marginalisation—a sort of "relic" of society—the face of a God who in his love for humanity had given up power and glory and humbled himself to step into the provisional nature of temporality and

31

finiteness. The crib and the cross were where God, in his Son, had chosen to show himself to the world; prior to the glory of the Resurrection, Jesus had wanted really to experience, in his own flesh, vulnerability, humiliation, and suffering.

Therefore Margaret accepted her pain as the sign of being specially chosen, and she lived in a beatitude of love that is the life of God himself in his Trinitarian relationship. In the long version of the *Legenda*, the key word is *paupertas*, which is not only being deprived of material goods but also marginalisation, precariousness, and uncertainty. This was not a state that Margaret chose freely, but just as she accepted sickness, abandonment, and betrayal with joyful detachment, so she accepted poverty as a gift that let her be wholly assimilated to Christ.

Thus, reread in the light of her *éscaton*, the poor, outcast girl's initial condition is reversed. As in the Magnificat, what corresponds to the annulment of every human power and benefit in Blessed Margaret is the gift of wisdom, as to her bodily blindness there corresponds the clarity of teaching, as to her ignorance there corresponds the luminous grace of the word, as to her lack of means and instruments there corresponds the power to perform miracles. So, the poor illiterate girl who knew nothing of books but had received everything from God became an esteemed spiritual teacher, made use of a charism generally associated with the learned and sometimes with prophets, although her witness was to remain more domestic and private, limited to the circle of her friends and spiritual daughters.

Unfortunately, the *Legenda* tends to leave her inner world in the background together with her ecstasies and visions, the mysteries that this Dominican virgin said she kept hidden in her heart. But she was a great mystic, comparable with those extraordinary figures—Angela of Foligno, Margaret of Cortona, Clare of the Cross, and Vanna of Orvieto—who in the fourteenth century, at a time of dreadful crisis in the history of the Church and of Europe, were "true priests of their towns" in the sacrifice and total offering of themselves, repeating with disarming literalism the evangelical figure of substitution. If, as Thomas Aquinas taught, Christ is the man "for others" come into the world for the redemption of humanity, these penitent women took on the same role as Christ for the salvation of souls.

Theirs was an endeavour limited to humble gestures but extremely significant in terms of what Christian commitment means in history, an action not based on power and money but carried out in caring for those who suffer in body and spirit; These women were able to love and keep intact their own spiritual freedom and the hope of the Gospel even in the face of the most crushing defeats and trials. This is the sign Margaret left to us, and this is why she has never been forgotten.

In the Light of the Word of God

Domenico Cancian
Bishop of Città di Castello

Every day Blessed Margaret went to the church of the Preachers, whose habit she wore, and when she had many confessors available, she wanted to make her confession daily, always hoping to receive a new infusion of grace by virtue of this sacrament. Every day she recited the Office of the Cross and of the Blessed Virgin and the entire Psalter, which she had miraculously learned. Blessed blind woman, I say, who never saw the things of this world yet who so quickly learned the heavenly things! Happy disciple, who merited to have such a master, who without books instructed in Holy Scripture. You, who were blind from birth, taught even those who see. In fact, we read of her that she listened to the children of Venturino and Grigia when they came home from school and corrected them when they made mistakes and sometimes wonderfully explained the verses of the Psalter.[21]

This text, which is also in the *Vita breve* (short life),[22] shows us how Blessed Margaret's spirituality was founded on the Word of God and not simply on the "devotions" that came from personal thoughts and feelings.

---

21. Vita lunga, 259.
22. Ibid., 299.

It is striking that she who was blind miraculously learned the entire Psalter. This is the gift of an infused wisdom that allowed her to pray with the inspired words, to understand them, and to live them and teach them. In this way she was imitating the Virgin Mary who listened, treasured, and meditated[23] on Scripture so that it became *"light for her steps."* The light and joy that shone from her sightless face came from the inspired Word that she bore in her heart, in her mouth, and above all in her life.

Praying the entire Psalter every day is a truly extraordinary commitment. In the whole Church tradition, this is the surest and most guaranteed way to live in communion with the Lord so that we can speak to Him in the words that He Himself suggested.

These words contain praise, thanksgiving, and requests for help, expressing all human feelings and willingness to listen to the Lord. The Psalms foster the encounter between the heart of God and the heart of man, as we find in the prayer that Jesus taught, addressed to the Father.

For Blessed Margaret, too, the words of Jesus are valid: "I thank you, Father, Lord of heaven and earth, because you have hidden these things from the wise and the intelligent and have revealed them to infants."[24] The Second Vatican Council recommended the faithful "to learn by frequent reading of the divine Scriptures the

---

23. Cf. Luke 2:19.
24. Matt. 11:25.

'excellent knowledge of Jesus Christ' so that God and Man may talk together."[25]

Christian holiness is based on constant, trusting prayer in the conviction that without Him we can do nothing, whereas with him we bear much fruit.[26]

Little Margaret, blind and illiterate, learned the inspired words and prayed with them. "Happy disciple, [...] blind from birth, who teaches even those who see."[27]

Blessed blind woman, who never saw the things of this world yet who so quickly learned the heavenly things. Happy disciple, who merited to have such a master, who without books instructed in Holy Scripture. You, who were blind from birth, who taught even those who see.[28]

---

25. Vatican II, *Dei Verbum*, 1965, no. 25.
26. Cf. John 15.
27. Vita lunga, 259.
28. L. Accattoli, Quando era facile la fede, in Il Regno, 2011.

Blessed Margaret and the Family

Giovanni Tani
Archbishop of Urbino-Urbania-Sant'Angelo in Vado

One of the most powerful messages that springs from the experiences Blessed Margaret lived through is linked to the family. Margaret had two family circles: her family of origin, well-off, in the Castle of Metola and the adoptive family that gave her a place to live in Città di Castello.

The anonymous author of the first biography of Margaret writes of her parents: "She was born of aristocratic parents, namely her father, Parisio, lord of the Castle of Metola in Massa Trabaria [...] while her mother was named Emilia; they, on seeing their daughter was blind, undersized, and deformed, struck with immense grief began to detest her."[29] Years after, in Città di Castello, "they abandoned her, without mercy, alone, without providing for her, with no human aid."[30] This was a very sad, painful affair, yet it did not prevent Providence from carrying out its plans. As she was growing up kept in isolation, a priest was close to this little girl, and he instructed her in faith and in prayer, laying the foundations in her of a spiritual life that was to reach such a level as to leave no trace in her soul of negative feelings towards her parents. The family who adopted Margaret in Città di Castello [Venturino eand

---

29. Vita lunga, 249.
30. Ibid., 253.

Grigia] "of one accord, through an inclination of charity, granted this poor girl, Margaret, a small cell in the upper part of their home, so that she might sleep there and devote herself to prayer."[31]

Two families that represent two opposing tendencies, one to rejection and the other to acceptance. It is difficult with our own criteria to judge the events that unfolded within the walls of the little castle of Metola: perhaps in some respects what occurred was like what happened until just a few years ago when people with disabilities were kept closed up in their homes. Looking at the matter as a whole, we may hazard the thought that the rejection might have taken the form of an abortion if it had been possible to know of the child's condition before she was born. Why should such a creature come into the world? What use is she? These are questions that push us too far, to the point of deciding on the existence of a living being. Thanks be to God that there are positive examples that give us pause for thought: among the many, we may remember what happened to Karol Wojtyla's parents who had to resist the advice of some doctors who advised abortion because of certain problems that had emerged. Their resistance and their faith, with the help of another doctor, ensured that the child who was to become St. John Paul II came into the world.

As for the family who took Margaret in, they fulfilled the vocation of reception in their hearts even before they

---

31. Ibid., 257.

gave her a place in their home. This is something very eloquent for our times: solidarity, care for the other, the ability to look at the other as a person beyond the limitations they present. It is a question of giving a family to one who has no family. We cannot fail to think of the many adoptions that are in our midst and of the children's homes where a family offers love and a place to live to so many who are in need.

The idea of family is undergoing a critical, problematic phase and its effects on society are emerging too. It must be said that society influences the family, and the family has an impact on society. The difficult period caused by the COVID-19 pandemic is putting families to the test, but beyond doubt it will be families that will guarantee the possibility for society to come through this period without splitting apart; however, they must not be left all alone. It is a fact that the family is "the beginning and basis of human society."[32] The historical facts of Blessed Margaret enlighten us on many aspects, both problematic and positive, of the family. Among them we must stress the vocation of the family to be protector of life: "the apostolate of married persons and families is of unique importance for the Church and civil society."[33] Venturino and Grigia offer a shining example of this apostolate.

---

32. Vatican II, *Apostolicam Actuositatem*, 1965, no. 11.
33. Ibid.

She Was Blind and
She Lived in Light

Luigi Accattoli

One afternoon, in the church of San Domenico in Città di Castello, I first saw Blessed Margaret's urn, and I had been drawn to her even in her remains, so small. She was blind, stunted, hunchbacked, and lame (her right leg was shorter than her left), and I spoke of her as the woman of the beatitudes: "Blessed are the poor, the afflicted, those who weep," and as one who, tormented, succours the tormented, Margaret becomes a highly relevant image of Gospel inversion. I recalled Luke 14:21: "Go out at once into the streets and lanes of the town and bring in the poor, the crippled, the blind, and the lame,"[34] and I said that she who was all of this, once she had gone to the banquet, laboured to drag in all the others who were forlorn. And that includes us.

I have told the story of the "legend" of Margaret following the reconstruction given by the Dominican historian William R. Boniwell in his short book *The Life of Blessed Margaret of Castello*.[35] The Italian edition is subtitled "vivere nella luce," living in light, as the mark of a blind woman's story. I first became interested in Margaret when I read this book and saw the image of her

---

34. Luke 14:21.
35. William R. Boniwell, *The Life of Blessed Margaret of Castello* (Rockford, IL: Tan Books and Publishers, 1983).

on its cover: there she is, her sight restored, with light emanating from her clear eyes. Ever since I learned to love this image, she has come to my aid when I pray Psalm 35: "In your light we see light."[36]

She is called "Margherita of Città di Castello" after the town where she died in 1320 or "Margaret of Metola" after a castle on the border between Umbria and the Marches where she was born in 1287. She is also called "the blind woman of Metola." She lived in various houses in Città di Castello and was admired for her sensitivity because she knew the Psaltery by heart and was even able to teach some Latin to seeing children despite her own blindness. Today we know how many things blind people can do. The author of the first biography of Margaret from the mid-fourteenth century has this to say about her skill as a teacher: "O blessed blind woman, who never saw the things of the world and who so quickly learned heavenly things. O happy disciple, who merited such a master who taught you, born blind and without books, to learn the Scriptures till you could teach the sighted." Providence enriched her with signs: one day a fire broke out in the Venturino family's house while she was upstairs in the attic she had chosen as her dwelling. They called to her to escape. She said calmly to Monna Gregoria, known as Grigia: "Take my cloak and throw it over the flames." The author of the legend describes this sign with words worthy of a dais designed by Simone Martini: "When Margaret's cloak was thrown

---

36. Psalm 35.

on the flames, the fire that had been roaring furiously went out immediately." [...] As for her Christian vocation, Margaret's story tells us that every period has its graces and disgraces. At that time people readily believed in miracles but had difficulty accepting the disabled and the different. We are ready to help our neighbour but slow to accept mystery. I believe that on the question of faith and charity, we are faced today with the need to overturn the traditional pedagogical course: in the past people started from faith, and in the name of faith in God they called believers to the duty of charity; today we should start from charity, which contemporary humanity can understand, and from that we should go back to faith in Him who is charity: *Deus caritas est*.

The Holiness of Blessed Margaret

Veronica Donatello and Fiorenza Pestelli

Reading the life of Blessed Margaret of Metola is not only interesting but above all modern because it offers the possibility of looking at disability from a new, up-to-date viewpoint.

Although she lived at the height of the Middle Ages, when disability was regarded as a disgrace and a divine curse, this woman, blind, hunchbacked, and lame, lived her entire life as a gift and as praise to God.

Segregated for a part of her life, abandoned by her original family, rejected by the convent, Margaret was able to bring the world a message of brim-full life, devoting her whole self to the needs of others, especially those most in need and cast out. This is how her life modeled a modern approach to the world of disability, as she became the protagonist of the choices made in her life, freeing herself from a society that saw her as defeated and cast out.

Pope Francis reminds us that "We are all called to be holy by living our lives with love and by bearing witness in everything we do, wherever we find ourselves."[37]

In fact, despite her numerous physical limitations, the voice of God exploded in her, accompanying her throughout her astonishing life, making her become the presence of divine mercy thanks to constant prayer, contemplation, and preaching of the Word of God.

---

37. Pope Francis, *Gaudete et Exsultate*, 2018, no. 14.

Her lay status, lived fully as a Dominican Tertiary of the Mantellate, leads us to rediscover the power and beauty of the Christian baptismal vocation because "following the principle of the incarnation of the Son of God, who is present in every human situation, the Church recognises in those with disabilities the call to faith and to a good life, full of meaning."[38]

This discovery of existential leadership offers the disabled the desire to fulfil the lofty magnitude of faith in belonging to Christ and at the same time transforms the church community into a place that generates life.

"A community that cherishes the little details of love, whose members care for one another and create an open and evangelizing environment, is a place where the risen Lord is present, sanctifying it in accordance with the Father's plan."[39]

Blessed Margaret triumphed in her challenge to society's marginalisation thanks to the acceptance and support of both the chaplain of the castle and Donna Grigia, who was able to sense in this creature all the potential she had. "Margaret is up-to-date because she was an authentic person, true to herself and aware of the power of the will and of faith; she accepted her life as a gift."[40] It was this self-knowledge that led her not to live

---

38. Rino Fisichella, *Direttorio per la Catechesi*, trans. (San Paolo Edizioni, Italy: 2020), no. 269.

39. Pope Francis, *Gaudete et Exsultate*, no. 145.

40. Sergio Campana and Ubaldo Valentini, *Il dono della Vita*, (Sant'Angelo in Vado: 2007), http://www.beatamargheritadellametola.it/down/vitabreve.pd

locked up in herself but rather to offer herself to others to testify joyfully to life, living without limits, accepting her existential condition.

As disciples of Christ, "we are called to be contemplatives even in the midst of action, and to grow in holiness by responsibly and generously carrying out our proper mission,"[41] and this is how Margaret lived out her commitment to and membership of the Church.

The encounter with God, which she sought tenaciously and kept in her heart, guided her to become a divine instrument of peace and joy for humanity, to seek to allay the sufferings of those close to her and to be a genuine expression of the mercy of the heavenly Father. In this way, Margaret became an example for humanity in our society which, promoting the "throwaway culture," marginalises those who are different, weak, or poor in favour of physical superiority, wholeness, and financial wellbeing.

Blessed Margaret's life reminds us that no one is self-sufficient and that no selfish casting off of others, whoever they may be, can lead to the genuine discovery of what we are and the authenticity of human beings.

The invitation her life suggests to us is that we cultivate a personal inner reality, discovered as a gift of love from the Father, to overcome the narcissistic attitude of selfish withdrawal with regard to the reality that is crushing today's world. The condition of a person

---

f

41. Pope Francis, *Gaudete et Exsultate*, no. 26.

with a disability calls us not to look on others only in terms of their deficiencies—the limitations everyone has—but on the contrary to embrace all the disharmonies of life in our own living.

Donna Grigia's welcoming her into the family is a testimony of inclusiveness that can direct and comfort the families of the disabled. In fact, from the documents on Margaret's life, there emerges the welcome and the urge towards human promotion that were shown by the entire family of Vittorino and Donna Grigia towards Margaret. They immediately made it possible to include her in the fabric of the family, integrating her in their children's studies and games and making her feel loved and admired.

They became her springboard so that she could be open to the town and to the poor and the outcast to the point that they helped her discover her vocation of total self-giving, and at the same time they became the promoters of a new culture of inclusion and acceptance for the society of their time. So, the way pointed out by Blessed Margaret of Metola leads us to rediscover our belonging to the people of God in that "sharing the word and celebrating the Eucharist together fosters fraternity and makes us a holy and missionary community. It also gives rise to authentic and shared mystical experiences."[42]

---

42. Ibid., no. 142.

Iconography of Blessed Margaret

Anna Fucili

The iconography and portrayals of Blessed Margaret reflect the hagiographic account of her life that was passed down by the two *legende* in Latin, summarised in a version in the Italian vernacular. There we read of her steadfast presence in the Dominicans' church in Città di Castello—she wore the Dominican habit and became a Tertiary—and above all, we read how after her death, her body, having been recovered, underwent an autopsy (as was customary at that time), and on that occasion three stones were found in the cardiac blood vessel, a phenomenon of "plastic stigmatisation" analogous to what was found, for example, in the heart of Santa Chiara (St. Clare) of Montefalco. These three "pebbles" bear the images of the Madonna (a lovely female figure with a golden crown), Jesus in the manger (a child in a crib surrounded by animals), and St. Joseph (a bald, white-bearded man with a golden cloak), in front of whom kneels a Dominican woman, Blessed Margaret, and on her side is the Holy Spirit, a pure white dove. One of the mysteries on which she most frequently meditated was, in fact, the mystery linked to the birth of Jesus and the motherhood and fatherhood of Mary and Joseph. As a result, her characteristic symbols are the habit of a Dominican Tertiary, a heart with three raised stones or pearls, the crib, the holy family, the lily, the crucifix, and sometimes a book—elements that characterise her when she is shown among other saints and blessed or

47

accompany her when she is the sole figure. One of the oldest images—in this case with a painted caption identifying her as "Beata Margarita dalla Città di Cast.", is to be found on the exquisite reredos *Beate domenicane: Giovanna da Firenze, Vanna da Orvieto, Caterina da Siena, Margherita da Città di Castello, Daniella da Orvieto*, the work of Andrea di Bartolo.[43] The figures are depicted on two levels. The upper level has the figures of Catherine of Siena—in the center, the only full-face portrayal—and the other four in profile. On the lower level, the same figures are shown at crucial moments of their lives: Giovanna in front of her home, saved from the flooding of the Arno; Daniella at the moment of her death, in ecstasy as two angels receive her soul; Vanna and Margaret praying before the crucified Jesus, like Catherine, who receives the stigmata. This work, commissioned by the Dominican Tommaso Caffarini who was from Siena, shows Catherine when she was still a blessed and hence with a radiated halo, making her like her companions, who had the same mystical experience—that Christocentric spirituality that relates them to the Crucified Lord.

Blessed Margaret is again portrayed with the cross and the lilies in two miniatures, initial block letters in

---

43. Andrea di Bartolo, Beate domenicane: Giovanna da Firenze, Vanna da Orvieto, Caterina da Siena, Margherita da Città di Castello, Daniella da Orvieto, 1394–1398, Venice, Academy Gallery.

the codex,[44] containing Caffarini's vernacular reworking of the Latin *legende*.

She is believed to be portrayed with other Dominican saints and blessed in the predella[45] of the *Fiesole Altarpiece* by Fra Angelico in the left-hand panel, one of the three Dominican women whose names are written on their habits. "*B. Ma(r)ga(r)ita*" is the last figure on the right, seen in profile, with a small heart in her left hand while golden rays emerge from her right hand. Some doubts remain as to whether this Blessed Margaret is really the tertiary of Città di Castello.

There is no doubt, however, of her identity in the painting attributed to Ludovico di Angelo Mattiloi, *Blessed Margherita of Città di Castello with Sts Margaret of Hungary and Agnes of Montepulciano*.[46] The heart with the three pearls in relief, together with the radiated halo, distinguishes her from the two saints with their respective features. All three hold the lily of purity and are identified by captions at the bottom.

Belonging to the Order reaches its crowning moment in the *Glory of the Dominican Order*,[47] shown as

---

44. Fifteenth century, Siena, city library.

45. Fra Angelico, *Fiesole Alterpiece*, 1423–1424, London, National Gallery.

46. Ludovico di Angelo Mattiloi, Blessed Margherita of Città di Castello with Sts Margaret of Hungary and Agnes of Montepulciano, fifteenth century, Perugia, National Gallery of Umbria.

47. Glory of the Dominican Order, eighteenth century,

crowded and complex: this work is distinguished not so much for its pictorial quality but for the detail regarding the "blind woman of Metola." It confirms a relationship recognised to her across the centuries and with a primary role which is confirmed by the painting. The figure of Margaret with the three-foiled heart is on the left in the middle part of the sequence introduced by St. Rose of Lima, who is embracing the bleeding feet of the crucified Jesus Christ. This is the central element, dominated by the golden light that radiates among clouds and angels from the empyrean heavens with the Virgin Mary, God the Father, and the dove of the Holy Spirit, while below them are the medallions of the mysteries of the Rosary.

Nor should we neglect two paintings in the Venetian convent building of SS Giovanni e Paolo (Saints John and Paul): in the sacristy, Margaret is portrayed on one of the lunettes devoted to the saints and blessed of the Order[48] and on a canvas[49] where she shows her tripartite heart, carries lilies, and is in prayer before the crib.

Devotion to this mediaeval mystic and penitent is always current, and this may lead to works that in their style put her in the context of her own time although carried out at a later date. This is the case of the triptych, thought to be of the Sienese school (Città di Castello,

Mesagne, Brindisi, Church of the Santissima Annunziata.

48. Leandro dal Ponte or Bassano, sixteenth century, Venice.

49. Leandro dal Ponte or Bassano, eighteenth century, Venice.

church of St. Dominic) but actually from the first half of the twentieth century: the figure of Margaret is shown in the section to the right of St. Dominic and shows the crib. On the opposite side is St. Catherine of Siena—three emblematic figures of the Order of Preachers.

Margaret can also be distinguished, again in company, this time with the saints of Città di Castello in the basilica there: *San Florido con Sant'Amanzio, San crescenziano, Sant'Illuminato e la Beata Margherita*,[50] (1697–1710), painted with lobed outlines in which, in one of the lobes, her Dominican figure emerges among the angels; *Madonna Assunta in Gloria tra angeli, I Santi di Città di Castello e la Beata Margherita*.[51] In this fresco, St. Florido the Bishop points to the small model of the city held by angels, partially covering St. Crescenziano, a Roman soldier and martyr, behind whom the priest St. Ventura is descending from on high with the axe of his martyrdom. In the adjacent group are the hermit St. Donnino (or Donino) and the priest St. Amanzio; and Blessed Margaret, in the Dominican habit, opens her arms and an angel offers her lilies and beside her is St. Veronica Giuliani, identifiable by her head crowned with thorns and her red heart in her hand. (This

---

50. San Florido con Sant'Amanzio, San crescenziano, Sant'Illuminato e la Beata Margherita, 1697–1710, Città di Castello.

51. Marco Benefial, Madonna Assunta in Gloria tra angeli, I Santi di Città di Castello e la Beata Margherita, 1747–1749, Città di Castello.

figure must have been added, since her beatification was in 1804 and her canonisation in 1839.)

There is no need of specific attributes or captions to identify Blessed Margaret when the story of her life and miracles is illustrated as with the case of the thirty-two lunettes frescoed in the cloister of the convent of St. Dominic in Città di Castello. These images make up the cycle carried out between 1662 and 1667 by Salvi Castellucci, a disciple of Pietro da Cortona, apart from five that are the work of Giovan Battista Pacetti, nicknamed "Lo Sguazzino" (the splasher). At the sides of each scene is a double caption in Latin and the vernacular summarising the episode portrayed from the birth of Margaret in 1287 to her miracles, concluding with the verification of the integrity of her body after her urn was opened in 1657; the body is preserved uncorrupted under the main altar of the church.

In this church there is also an illustrated *legenda*, this time in twelve squares, in the glass panel installed in 1914 by the Quentin company of Florence, designed by the Parisian Francesco Mossmayer, with the other which shows her alone. There are several portrayals of Margaret on glass: in Mercatello on the Metauro in the same years and by the same author in the church of San Francesco; by Rita Rivelli in 1997 in the collegiate of Saints Peter and Paul; and one more at Sant'Angelo in Vado in the church of San Michele arcangelo (St. Michael the archangel, 1930), where she is shown with Blessed Girolamo Ranuzzi. In most cases, she is a solitary figure in her own panel but not alone: beside her is St. Veronica

Giuliani, following an established custom—as in the statues on the façade of the church of San Cristoforo (St. Christopher) in Urbania or San Giacomo apostolo (St. James the Apostle) in Calvizzano, Naples—of putting side by side the images of these two mystics who lived in the same places, in the two dioceses of Urbino and Città di Castello. This sustains a special link that reaches its peak in the patron saint of Urbino, San Crescenziano, later known as San Crescentino. Margaret too is known by two names, Margaret of Metola or of Città di Castello, which seems to be comprehensive, but she is named in accordance with the origin of the works and artistic objects linked to one or the other territory; these objects are the fruit of her cult, and their presence in various places in Italy and around the world make her a "global" figure, not confined to limited environments such as where she was born or who adopted her.

At Sant'Angelo in Vado there are two paintings: *San Biagio e la Beata Margherita della Metola* (church of Santa Caterina al corso [St. Catherine on the road], seventeenth/eighteenth century) and *Madonna con Bambino, San Domenico, il Beato Girolamo Ranuzzi e la Beata Margherita della Metola* (Madonna with Child, St. Dominic, Blessed Jerome Ranuzzi, and Blessed Margherita della Metola, church of San Michele arcangelo [St. Michael the Archangel], 1860) which draw attention to the heart with three conspicuous signs, the lily, and in both cases, a red book in her hand or on the ground. Mercatello sul Metauro, which has her monument in the public gardens and an altar with a papier-mâché statue by Giuseppe Malecore facing the statue of St. Veronica in the collegiate church of SS Pietro e Paolo (Saints Peter and Paul), preserves paintings which, together, seal the iconographic features of the Dominican virgin: the lily, the heart with three pearls, and the "crib." Exemplarily, in the church of Santa Chiara (St. Clare), there is a canvas (eighteenth/nineteenth century) showing Margaret with the elements of the tripartite, engraved heart, and the lily while the caption along the base expresses gratitude to the Holy Family, Jesus, Mary, and Joseph: "Margarita Deo Genuit Tres Grata Mariam et Jesum st Joseph Mira Ter Acta Parens"; here too is the painting of St. Veronica Giuliani (nineteenth century).

Bibliography

Accattoli, L. *Quando era facile la fede*. In *Il Regno*, 2011.

Angelico, Fra. *Fiesole Alterpiece*. 1423–1424. London, National Gallery.

Benefial, Marco. *Madonna Assunta in Gloria tra angeli, I Santi di Città di Castello e la Beata Margherita*. 1747–1749. Città di Castello.

Bonniwel, William R. *Margherita di Città di Castello, Vivere nella luce*. Rome: Città Nuova Editrice, reissue 2002.

Boniwell, William R. *The Life of Blessed Margaret of Castello*. Rockford, IL: Tan Books and Publishers, 1983.

Campana, Sergio and Ubaldo Valentini. *Il dono della Vita*. Sant'Angelo in Vado: 2007. http://www.beatamargheritadellametola.it/down/vitabreve.pdf

Di Angelo Mattiloi, Ludovico. *Blessed Margherita of Città di Castello with Sts Margaret of Hungary and Agnes of Montepulciano*. Fifteenth century. Perugia, National Gallery of Umbria.

Di Bartolo, Andrea. *Beate domenicane: Giovanna da Firenze, Vanna da Orvieto, Caterina da Siena, Margherita da Città di Castello, Daniella da Orvieto*. 1394–1398. Venice, Academy Gallery.

Fisichella, Rino. *Direttorio per la Catechesi*. Translated. San Paolo Edizioni, Italy: 2020.

GiovaGnoli, E. *Vita della beata Margherita da Città di Castello, Terziaria domenicana*. Città di Castello: Tipografia Petruzzi, reissue 1997.

Glory of the Dominican Order. Eighteenth century. Mesagne, Brindisi, Church of the Santissima Annunziata.

Lécu, Anne and Valerio Lanzarini. *Una vita donata*. Magnano (BI): Qiqajon, 2018.

Licciardello, P. *Le vite dei santi di Città di Castello*. Selci Lama: Editrice Pliniana, 2017.

Pessoa, Fernando. *Sono un sogno di Dio*. Magnano (BI): Qiqajon, 2015.

Pope Francis. *Gaudete et Exsultate*. 2018.

San Florido con Sant'Amanzio, San crescenziano, Sant'Illuminato e la Beata Margherita. 1697–1710. Città di Castello.

Valentini, U. *Beata Margherita della Metola, Una sfida all'emarginazione*. Città di Castello: Tipografia Petruzzi, 1988.

Vatican II. *Dei Verbum*. 1965.

Vita lunga della Beata Margherita (Recensio major, BHL 5313az). In Le vite dei santi di Città di Castello nel Medioevo, edited by P. Liccardello, 251–261. Selci-Lama, Italy: Editrice Pliniana, 2017.